40 Studies for Clarinet
BOOK ONE

by
CYRILLE ROSE

with editing and Master Lessons by
Dr. DONALD E. McCATHREN

This edition is dedicated to
James Paterson

EL 03457

Editorial assistance: Jack Lamb and Mark Johnson
Cover and design: Warren E. Conway

ABOUT THE COMPOSER
CYRILLE ROSE (1830-1902)

I am indebted to Dr. David Pena, Professor of Clarinet at Southwest Texas State University, for sending me the information about the life of Cyrille Rose. I am also indebted to Pamela Westen and her book, *More Clarinet Virtuosi of the Past,* from which this information is taken.

Rose, a Frenchman, was born in Lestren, France. He studied under Klose at the Paris Conservatoire, receiving First Prize in 1847. Although he is mainly known as a teacher, he was also a fine performer. He had a beautiful tone and artistic phrasing. The only concert tour he is known to have undertaken was in 1852 when he toured Germany.

Rose played in the opera orchestra from 1857 to 1891. The clarinet parts still retain the many slurs he added, for he had a sluggish tongue. Gounod and Massenet frequently consulted him on technical points. Rose also played for the Société des Concerts from 1857 to 1872.

He was particularly fond of the Weber Concertos and performed one of them for the Société in 1862. He made excellent editions of Weber's compositions and supplied the concertos with cadenzas.

Rose was Professor at the Paris Conservatory from 1876, until he retired in 1900. He then went to teach at the conservatory in Meaux. He was said to be a most devoted teacher. Among his students are the following well-known players: Cahuzac, Manuel and Francisco Gomez, Jeanjean, Henri Lefebre, Paradis, Henri and Alexandre Selmer (founders of the Selmer Company), Strevenard and Verney.

Rose collaborated with the Buffet Company in experiments with the width of bore and the cones at the top and bottom of the clarinet. He was awarded the Legion of Honor by the French Government in 1900.

Cyrille Rose is well known for his sets of *40 Studies* and *32 Studies.* Both books are excellent and prove Rose to be very talented as a composer, as well as a clarinetist. The *32 Studies* are not original, but are transcriptions of some of the *48 Studies* for oboe by Ferling. They are excellent transcriptions and are a fine addition to the clarinet repertoire. The studies in this collection are taken from his *40 Studies.*

Dr. Donald E. McCathren

ABOUT THE EDITOR
DR. DONALD E. McCATHREN

Dr. Donald E. McCathren has spent a lifetime studying and teaching clarinet. He began his clarinet career at the age of 12 in Hobart, Indiana where his first music teacher was Dr. William D. Revelli. Other clarinet teachers while at Hobart included Dal Fields, Lee Christman, Louis Greenspan, Bertram Francis, and Fred Ebbs. While in high school, he was selected to be the solo clarinetist of the Carilco Concert Band. This professional band was under the sponsorship of the U. S. Steel Corporation.

Among other teachers have been Daniel Bonade of the Philadelphia Orchestra, Victor Polatschek of the Boston Symphony, Harley Froman of the U.S. Navy Band, Angelo DeCapria of the Detroit Symphony, and Albert Friedman of the Chicago Civic Symphony.

Dr. McCathren has studied at Indiana State University, Indiana University, Tufts University, Chicago Musical College, and the U.S. Navy School of Music.

He has appeared in all 50 states as a clarinet soloist, conductor, or clarinet clinician. He has also made appearances in Eastern and Western Europe, South Africa, Japan, Okinawa, Bermuda, and the Bahama Isles. He has served on the clinical staffs of the G. Leblanc Corp., Selmer Corp., and the Armstrong Company.

The music magazine, THE SCHOOL MUSICIAN, selected 70 of the most outstanding musicians who have done the most for American music in the past 50 years. Dr. McCathren was among the 70.

He has appeared widely as a clarinet soloist, chamber music artist, and in bands and orchestras. He was solo clarinetist of the Greater Boston Service Man's Symphony, which was conducted by Arthur Fiedler. He was also one of the solo clarinet players in the U.S. Navy Broadcast Band in Washington, D.C. during World War II.

He has taught clarinet and/or woodwinds at Indiana University, Indiana State University, Chicago Musical College, and Duquesne University. He has appeared as a part-time faculty member at 42 additional colleges and universities and at countless clinics and workshops.

In addition, he is the president, founder, and musical director of the American Youth Symphony, Band, and Chorus, conducting bands and orchestras on annual good will summer concert tours.

USE OF THE MASTER LESSON PLANS

Each exercise has been provided with a master lesson plan to assist the student in learning to play the exercise.

In playing the exercises, the student will note that some of the measure numbers have been circled. This indicates that the measure has a helpful comment listed in the Master Lesson plan under that measure number.

Special signs have also been included in the music. Among these are:

⌐ = Keep the right hand down   L = Use the left hand little finger   ⅃ = Use the forked fingering (T, 1, 4)

R = Use the right hand little finger   ⌒ = Slide

Numerous expression and phrasing marks have been added to make the exercises more musical. When a student has the good fortune of studying with an experienced teacher, and there is a disagreement in the method where something is being taught, the student should by all means use the teacher's suggestions.

There are many ways of playing the clarinet and solving clarinet problems. The editor has presented the solutions that are deemed best in his experience; but, there are many answers to all problems so that these are to serve merely as guides. The presence of an artist teacher is always preferred to any book, including this one.

Rhythm problems in this work are explained using a system correlated to the movement of the foot in counting time. The system uses only the words "down" and "up" combined with numbers. In counting using this system, an arrow down is used to indicate a down beat, and an arrow up to indicate an upbeat. It is suggested that the student practice counting and tapping following this time counting chart.

STUDY No. 1

This is one of the most beautiful exercises from the entire 40 Studies. It should be noted that players of the Eb soprano, alto, bass and contrabass clarinet may study these exercises with equal benefit. The purpose of this exercise is to develop a smooth and connected legato fingering technique both in scales and extended intervals. This is extremely important to the development of artistic slow playing on the clarinet.

The "Allegretto cantabile" indicates that the exercise is to be played in a light, cheerful, melodious and graceful style. The ♩ = 76 indicates that there should be 76 quarter notes per minute. This tempo can be found by setting a metronome to 76 or by using a slightly faster tempo than the second ticked off by a watch.

To obtain the best benefit of this study it is suggested that in the beginning it be played twice as slow or ♪ = 76. After the exercise has been mastered, gradually increase the tempo to ♩ = 76.

Measure 1. The Italian word "dolce" indicates that the exercise is to be played in a sweet, delicate style.

There are two general types of finger technique used in playing the clarinet. When playing rapid passages the fingers move quickly like little hammers. In slow passages the fingers move slowly causing the tone to bend connecting from one tone to the next. This is a portamento style (carrying across). One of the main purposes is to develop this slow legato method of finger technique. A basic fingering technique on the clarinet is holding the fingers of the right hand down while playing the throat register. The sign ⌐⌐ indicates that the right hand may be held down across the throat tones. Keeping the right hand down across the tones G, G#, A and A# makes the passages smoother and more easily played. It is suggested that this fingering technique not be used in the slow study of this exercise in order to better obtain the legato training for the fingers. It is however important that the student realize that this fingering technique is available and highly recommended, particularly on fast passages.

Measure 2. In playing this measure, move the fingers slowly and make certain there are no breaks between the notes. If there should be a problem between notes, repeat the notes slowly over and over until the problem is eliminated.

The sign " ⁊ " is a phrase or breath mark. It indicates the end of a musical sentence, or a place where a breath may be taken, or both.

Measure 6. The notes going up the scale are more important than the notes that remain the same. The notes going up the scale are to be played with a crescendo as they are a melody leading to the top note C. The moving notes may be thought of as the melody and repeated notes as the accompaniment.

Measure 9. There are two ways to finger the first space F# on the clarinet. One is with the thumb and the two lower side keys. This fingering is only used in chromatic passages from the thumb F to the F#. The other fingering for this F# is with the first finger of the left hand. In measure 9 and at all other times in this exercise this F# is to be fingered with the first finger of the left hand.

Measure 12. When there are long notes in a phrase they must be given life with either a crescendo or a decrescendo. If the note is moving toward a climax it will be given a crescendo. If it is moving toward a repose, it will be given a decrescendo. In this measure the half-note B is moving to the first note in the following measure. It should therefore be given a crescendo. As you perform look for similar expressive notes and play them in a similar fashion.

Measure 13. The first note of this measure is the climax of the phrase that began in measure 12. This note should be played a little longer and a little louder to indicate the climax.

Measure 14. The letter "R" under the "C#" indicates that the "C#" is to be fingered with the right little finger. Playing this note with the right little finger keeps the fingering in one hand for better coordination. There are other passages where the right hand little finger is recommended.

Measure 16, 17 and 18. The "cresc. poco a poco" means to get gradually louder. That is, "Crescendo little by little".

Measure 19. In playing the high D and other notes in the high register better control can be obtained by half-holing. In this technique, the high D is played by rolling the first finger of the left hand down to open the upper half of the first tone hole. The D can then be prevented from popping out of the clarinet with excessive volume.

Measure 20. In playing music some notes are more important than others. These notes are sometimes indicated by a tenuto mark (—) as has been done in this measure. The notes under the tenuto mark may be brought out by playing them longer, louder or both. Playing other passages in a similar fashion will help to give an interesting musical performance.

Measure 21. The "dim. poco rit." means to get softer and a little slower.

Measure 22. The words "A Tempo" mean to return to the tempo before it was changed by the "poco rit."

Measure 29. The high D should crescendo all the way to the C in measure 30.

Measure 31. The three grace notes are played lightly, quickly and just ahead of the third beat.

Measure 40. Play the arpeggio with a small ritard to give a more finished effect. The third space C should be played with the right little finger to keep the fingering in one hand.

Measure 41. Hold the C at a full fortissimo level. Do not decrescendo. For a very dramatic ending, draw the air in to stop the tone. This is an inhaled release.

40 STUDIES
for
CLARINET

by C. ROSE.
edited by Donald McCathren

BOOK I

Grade III

6

STUDY No. 2

Moderato ♩ = 96 indicates an easygoing moderate tempo. To practice this exercise at the correct tempo set a metronome at 96. This will result in 96 beats per minute. When first practicing the exercise, however, it is suggested that a slower tempo of about ♩ = 70 be used. This will make it possible for the player to become accustomed to the new fingerings and also the various fingering patterns of the exercise without making many errors.

It is suggested that the exercise be practiced with the fullest tone and also the softest possible tone. Playing *mf* on the instrument is easy. Playing the extremes in volume however, is difficult. Thus we can prepare ourselves to play the difficult extremes in other music by practicing this exercise at the extremes. To make the dynamics more interesting, alternate each line between *ff* and *pp*.

The letters R and L indicate that the right or left little fingers should be used.

When a passage causes difficulties, slow it down and then practice it over and over getting gradually faster. Practicing a passage incorrectly leads to poor playing rather than the excellence we all seek.

Measure 1. The sign ⌐ indicates that the right hand may be held down across the throat tone G. The third-line Bs should be fingered with the right little finger.

Measure 2. The B should be played with the right little finger in this measure. The sign " ❜ " at the end of the measure indicates that the last notes should be tapered (═►) and a breath taken at the end of the measure.

Measure 3. When holding the right hand down across the open Gs it is best to lift the 6th and little fingers when playing the second G to prepare for the E that follows.

Measure 8. Playing the high notes (C to G above the staff) are difficult on the clarinet. These notes have a strong tendency to sound harsh and to come out too loud. The tone quality and volume of these notes can be greatly improved by fingering the first tone hole half-holed. Thus the E in this measure would be played in this fashion. The sign " ½ " is used to indicate this fingering. Be certain to open the top of the tone hole.

Measure 9. Play the 1st third line B with the right little finger. Play the next B with the right little finger on C and the left little on the B key. This prepares the following C to be played with the right little finger.

Measure 11. This passage may be greatly facilitated by playing the Eb with the forked fingering (T 1 4). The sign for this is the numbers $\frac{1}{4}$. The first finger of the right hand (4) should be held down across the open Gs. Make special note of the key change to Bb Major.

Measure 13. The high Eb's should be played half-hole in this measure. The first line Eb should be played with the forked fingering (T 1 4).

Measure 14. The Eb's in this measure would be played using the standard fingering (T 1 2 Eb). The Eb key is the bottom side key.

Measure 15. Finger the C with the left little finger so that the Eb's can be played with the right little finger.

Measure 21. Note the key change to G major.

Measure 22. The fermata (hold) (⌢) over the sixteenth rest indicates a silent pause. To make this measure sound more musical it is suggested that a ritard be made leading to the pause.

Measure 31. The first middle-line B in this measure should be played with the right little finger. The second B should be played with the right little finger on the C key and the left little finger on the B key. This prepares the fingers for playing the second C in the third beat of the measure.

Measure 36. The Italian word "poco" means little. Thus a small ritard would be used to create and artistic ending to the exercise.

Practice carefully, for the clarinet habits of a lifetime are being built today.

Grade III

Nº 2

STUDY No. 3

Moderato ♩= 96.   This indicates a moderate easy tempo, not fast and not slow.

When first practicing this exercise, it is recommended that a tempo half as fast be used. This would be 96 eighth notes per minute. It is best to practice at least part of the time using a metronome.

The purpose of this study is to develop the ability to play wide intervals both slurred and tongued. Practice *ff* and *pp* to develop dynamic control.

When playing larger intervals, it is extremely important to "focus" the throat, mouth, tongue and embouchure for each note as it is played. All of the vowel sounds should be used.

Measure 1. The chalumeau (low) G should be played as if saying "oo" while the clarion B (third line) would be played as if saying "ah". The notes in measure 2 would be played in the same fashion.

Measure 5. The clarion (third space) C# should be fingered using the R F# - C# key.

Measure 6. Finger the D# with the T 1 5 fingering.

Measure 7. The F# should be fingered with the first finger of the left hand.

Measure 10. Slurring from A to C and G# to B is very difficult and requires perfect coordination. These two intervals should be isolated and practiced repeatedly until they are mastered. Be sure to roll onto the A and G# keys.

Measure 12 and 13. The throat tones A and G# can be played with the right hand down. The F# should by played with the right hand little finger.

Measure 13. Since the low G# can only be played with the right little finger, the B must be played with the left little finger.

Measure 14. Playing the C# with the right little finger keeps the fingering in one hand and thus improves coordination.

Measure 16. This C# must be played on the left as the G# that follows can only be played on the right.

Measure 18. The grace note should be played an instant before the third beat. Grace notes should be played quickly and lightly. They get no time value.

Measure 19. The grace note F# should be played an instant before the second beat. The high D should be played half-hole and as if saying the syllable "ee".

Measure 24. The high Bb can best be executed using the "forked" fingering T (thumb) R (register) and fingers 1 and 4.

Measure 25. The accents should be made with a burst of air rather than by tonguing harder.

Measure 26. The low F should be played with the right little finger. The grace note should be played just ahead of the top line F.

Measure 29. Start the accented notes louder and then play the note that follows at the normal dynamic level. See measure 25 for additional comments. Keep the 5th finger from the low G# down across the throat G# to the low B.

Measure 38. The third line B should be played with the left little finger so the right little finger can be used to play the high D. The notes from high C# to high G can be played with greater control if the first finger of the left hand is rolled down opening half of the first tone hole. The sign for this is "½" which means half-hole.

Measure 39. The C# would also be played half-hole. These high notes often pop out too loudly. Playing them half-hole helps to avoid an unpleasant sound.

Measure 51. The high Bb here would be best played using the standard Bb fingering (TR12Eb) (thumb, register key, 1st and 2nd fingers left hand and the bottom side key).

Measure 62. The high D and E should be played half-hole. This will make it possible to play these notes with excellent control so they can be played *pp* when practicing at this dynamic level.

Measure 69. A slight ritard would be desirable in this measure to give the exercise a greater feeling of finality.

Careful, excellent practice leads to beautiful artistic clarinet playing.

Grade II

No 3.

STUDY No. 4

This study has been written to develop smoothness in playing scales, thirds, and broken chords. The editor has added dynamics including crescendos and dimenuendos to correspond with the rise and fall of the lines in the study. This will assist the young player in obtaining a more musical performance. The tempo Allegro ♩ = 144 is very rapid. It is suggested that a tempo of half of that speed be used in the beginning when learning this study. Gradually increase the tempo until ♩ = 144 has been reached. The breath markings have been added to guide the student. The ones inside circles are for use when practicing slowly. Those without circles are for use when playing at faster tempos.

Measure 1. Finger the B with the right little finger on C and the left little finger on B.

Measure 2. The line over the high B is a tenuto marking. Play this note a little longer to indicate the climax of the phrase.

Measure 11. The first B should be played wtih the right little finger. This keeps the fingering here all in the right hand for better coordination. Play the following third line B with the right little finger on C and the Left little finger on B. This prepares the fingers for the C that follows.

Measure 12. Finger the C# with the right hand little finger to keep the fingering in the right hand.

Measure 16. Finger the C# with the left hand little finger.

Measure 20. The D# may be best played with the forked fingering (T 1 4), that is, the thumb and the first finger of each hand. The sign for this is ¼

Measure 21. The sign ⌐⌐ is a reminder to keep the right hand down across the throat register. In this case the two fingers from the right hand of low A are held down across the A and G# to the B. Then the three fingers of the right hand are held down across A to the C#.

Measure 27. The first space F# should be fingered with the first finger of the left hand both times it appears.

Measure 29. The E trill should be prepared by starting slowly and getting gradually faster. The E should be trilled to the note above in the key, which is F#.

Measure 31. The D# should be fingered with the forked fingering using Thumb and fingers 1 and 5. This sets up the fingering for the B natural that follows.

Measure 32. All of the third space C# s in this measure should be played with the right little finger. The sign ⌐⌐ indicates that the first finger of the right hand should be held down from the D across the A and the 5th line F#.

Measure 35. Play the first note with the chromatic fingering (T R 1 2 3 4 B). This sets up the high D fingering that follows.

Measure 39. The hold over the 32nd rest indicates that a pause is to made at this point. It gives the player the opportunity to get ready for the flourish that follows.

Measure 40. The word "Presto" means to play quickly or very rapidly. This makes for a very exciting ending to the study.

Measure 44. The Tenuto marks in this measure indicate that the notes are to be played legato.

Learn to select and adjust your reeds. Remember, a clarinetist is only as good as his reed.

Grade IV

Nº 4

STUDY No. 5

This is an exercise intended for the development of stopped staccato, slurred small intervals and short crescendos and decrescendos. If the student is not familar with the technique of stopped staccato an explanation is due. To play stopped staccato, stop the tone with the tongue while continuing to blow. This will make a brilliant short note. Stopped staccato can be executed by saying the word "tut". This form of tonguing should only be used in fast passages with short notes. To use it in slow passages will result in an unmusical sound at the end of the notes.

Allegro means lively. Set the metronome at ♩ = 126 to find the correct tempo for this exercise.

Measure 1. Play the first note of each beat very short using stopped staccato. Make a controlled crescendo in two beats with the climax of the crescendo on the first note of the third beat. An even decrescendo follows for the remainder of the measure. It is difficult to make an even two beat crescendo and a two beat diminuendo. It should be mentioned that the editor has added these dynamics to make the exercise more challenging and beneficial.

Measure 6. The sign ⌐¬ means to hold the right hand down (or parts of it). Finger the second B with the chromatic fingering (T 1 2 3 4 B). This fingering makes this passage easier to finger.

Measure 7. The first B♮ should also be fingered with the chromatic fingering.

Measure 8. The word "similar" means to continue the dymanics that preceded in the measures just played. Finger the Db each time with the right little finger on C and the left little finger on C#.

Measure 10. It is suggested that the student try playing the Gb both with the first finger left hand and with the thumb and two bottom side keys. Each fingering has its merits and drawbacks. Use the one that works best. The editor prefers the fingering using the first finger left hand but either one is acceptable.

Measure 12. C flat is the same note as B♮. Play all the C flats in this measure with the right little finger.

Measure 14. It is suggested that the first Eb be fingered using the forked fingering (T 1 4).

Measure 16. The Db should be fingered with the right little finger on C and the left little finger on the C# key. The high Bb would be fingered with the forked fingering (T R 1 4).

Measure 17. This measure is the same as measure 16. The same fingerings are suggested.

Measure 21. It is suggested that the C# be fingered with the right little finger to keep the fingering in one hand. The Eb would be fingered using the forked fingering (T 1 4).

Measure 25. Note the key change to D Major. The rule for knowing the name of the Major key is that the note above the last sharp is the name of the key.

Measure 29. It is suggested that the third line B be fingered with the right little finger in order to keep the fingering in one hand.

Measure 33. It is suggested that the C#s in this measure be fingered with the right little finger to keep it in the right hand. It is recommended that the high C# be fingered half hole.

Measure 35. The accent in this and the following measures should be made with a small burst of air rather than tonguing heavier. It sometimes helps to think of playing the note *ff* and then after it has been started at this dynamic level, to continue the note at the dynamic being used. It is suggested that the high D be played with the half hole to avoid having it sound too loudly.

Measure 45. Measures 45 and 46 are the climax of the long crescendo indicated by the "cresc. poco a poco" (louder, little by little). It is suggested that the middle B and C be fingered with the right little finger. Fingering the high C# and high D half hole will help them to sound at a volume even with the surrounding notes.

The habits of a lifetime are being formed today. Make certain the habits you are making lead to excellence.

Grade III

poco a poco cresc.

STUDY No. 6

This is one of the most delightful studies of the entire 40. It shows the outstanding originality and great playing skills that C. Rose possessed. The purpose of the study is to develop quickness of tongue and fingers in playing 32nd notes. The editor has added the expression markings to give the student additional challenge and to make the study more musical.

Moderato ♩ = 92 indicates a moderate tempo.

Measure 1. The word "leger" means to play the exercise in a light and nimble style. Play the 32nd notes very lightly and quickly just ahead of the note that follows. Make certain that the 32nd note goes to the note that follows and that this note receives the emphasis. It is suggested that the stopped staccato style of tonguing be used.

Measure 2. Hold the first finger of the right hand down across open G to the top line F that follows. This is indicated by the sign ⌐⌐

Measure 3. The comma indicates that this would be a good place to take a breath.

Measure 6. Finger the F# with the first finger of the left hand. The same fingering should be used for the F# in measure 7.

Measure 7. The letters R and L indicated the little fingers that are to be used. The first note (B) would be fingered with the right little finger on C and the left little finger on B.

Measure 11. Finger the first note (F#) with the right little finger. Hold the right hand down across the A's as indicated by the sign ⌐⌐ .

Measure 14. Note the change in dynamic patterns. Since the musical patterns have changed, the dynamic patterns have changed to suit the music.

Measure 16. Note the change in dynamics. The fourth note (C) would be fingered on the right and the following two Bs with the right little finger on C and the left little finger on B.

Measure 18. While the first B is fingered with the right little finger, the second B is fingered with the right little finger on C and the left little finger is on B. The following two Bs would be fingered similarly.

Measure 21. The 4th and 5th fingers of the right hand would be held down across the Bb and G to the following E.

Measure 28. There is a change of rhythm in this measure. Instead of counting 6 notes to the beat there are now only four notes. Count these notes "Down 2 3 4" to obtain the correct rhythm.

Measure 29. Return to counting "Down 2 3 4 5 6 "in this measure.

Measure 30. If this C should be a little flat, open the bottom side key to bring it into tune.

Remember, don't practice faster than you can play perfectly.

Grade IV

Nº 6

STUDY No. 7

This is one of the most beautiful of the Rose Studies. Its purpose is to develop the ability to play smooth even chordal passages and well-controlled trills. When all practicing has been completed, the study is to be played with two beats to the measure. The indication of "Allegro moderato ♩ = 96" means a less than lively tempo or moderately lively. Until the fingers have mastered the fingering patterns as well as the trills, it is suggested that the exercise be practiced in four beats to the measure with a quarter note getting 96 beats per minute. Later, play the exercise in two at ♩ = 96.

Measure 1. The dynamics suggested in the first and second measures are those of the editor. It is suggested that the clarinetist use dynamics as the exercise is practiced to make the exercise more musical and more musically demanding.

Measure 3. Holding the first finger of the right hand down across the two As and the Bb aids in keeping the right hand in good position and makes the D more easily played.

Measure 4. When slur follows slur, play the slurs legato for a better musical effect.

Measure 11. It is suggested that the Bb be fingered with the forked fingering (T R 1 4). This will make it much easier to finger the E that follows.

Measure 12. The grace notes should be played quickly, lightly and just ahead of the first beat of the measure.

Measure 14. Finger the grace note C by holding the Bb and touching the two top side keys to produce the C.

Measure 15. To trill from F to G hold the F and trill with the G# key.

Measure 16. There is a misprint in this measure in most editions. The grace notes should be F# and G. The corrections have been made in this edition.

Measure 17. Trill the A to Bb by holding the A and trilling with the second from the top side trill key. This is the Bb key. To simplify the trill from Eb to F make the trill just by moving the second finger of the right hand.

Measure 18. The Bb should be trilled to C just as was done in fingering the C grace note in measure 14. That is, hold the Bb and trill with the two top side keys.

Measure 44. The technique of holding the right hand, or part of it, down across the throat register works the same for notes below the throat register as well as those above. (See measure 6).

Measure 47. The crescendo and decrescendo markings are those of Rose. The other dynamic markings in the remainder of the piece are also his . . . with the exception of the dynamics in the first two measures.

Measure 51. In this and the following measures Rose has given us both a phrase indication and an articulation indication. The long mark is the phrase indication. The short marks indicate the articulation.

Measure 56. It is suggested that the high D be played with the ½ hole fingering to avoid having this note sound too loudly.

Measure 59. It is suggested that the C# be fingered with the left C# key. Be sure to play C# in the 16th note triplet. To make the rhythm accurate, subdivide the beat into 4 parts. Count "Down 2, 3, 4". Play the trill on three parts of the beat and the triplet on the 4th part.

Measure 70. Hold the first finger of the right hand down across the G#. Finger the Bb with the forked fingering and play the B natural with the right little finger.

Measure 78. Rose has once again given us both articulation and phrase markings. Observe both indications. The "poco rit." has been added by the editor to give a musical ending to the exercise.

Be sure to practice slowly and carefully when learning new fingering patterns. Repeat each one over and over until it has been engrained into your mind and muscles. Remember, slow careful practice is the key to fine, artistic clarinet playing.

Grade III

No. 7

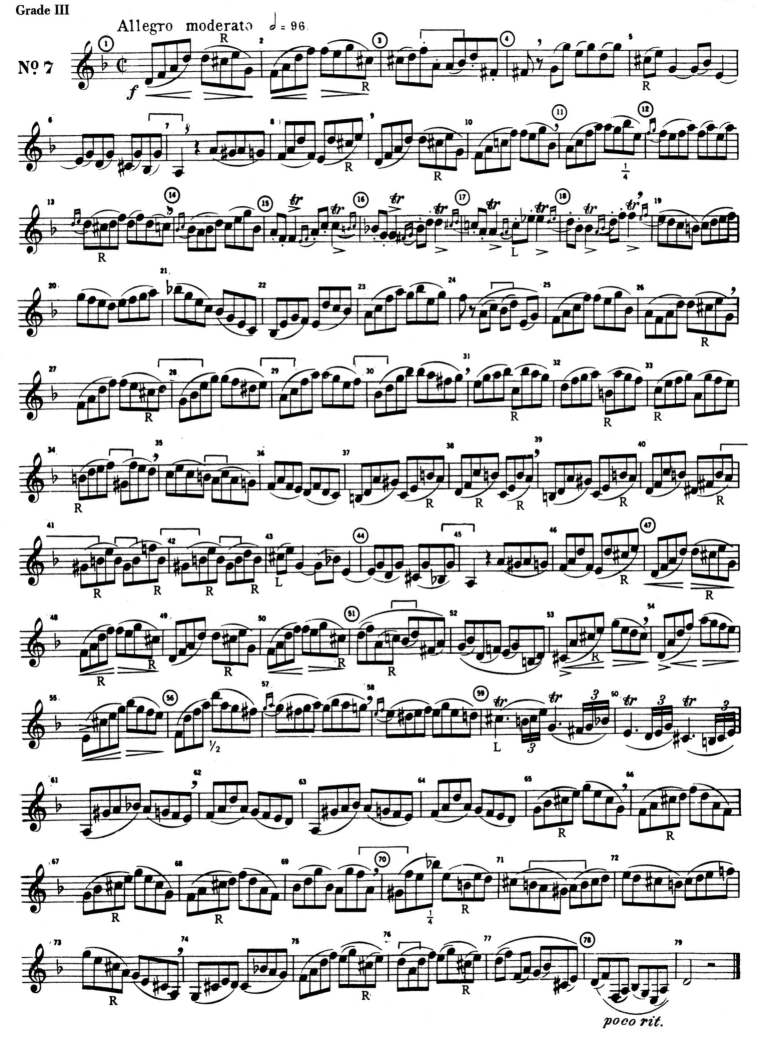

poco rit.

STUDY No. 8

The purpose of this exercise is to develop the triplet feeling, to practice making an excellent accent, to further improve the stopped staccato and to work on dynamic control. The feeling for the triplet is put to test in several measures where the notes are slurred in groups of two across the triplet. Measure 36 is an example of this.

Measure 1. Make the accents with a small puff of air rather than with the tongue. It is sometimes helpful to start the notes with the accent one or two dynamics louder and then to drop back to the dynamic level being used.

Measure 2. The sign ⌐⌐ indicates to keep the right hand down from the B in the 1st measure across the A and G to the first B in measure two. The R means to finger the Bs with the right little finger.

Measure 3. The accent marks were left out of this measure in error. The editor has added them.

Measure 6. The letters L and R here mean to play the B with the right little finger on the C key and the left little finger on the B key.

Measure 9. Rose begins using staccato markings with this measure. It is suggested that the technique of stopped staccato be used. In this style of tonguing the note is stopped with the tongue while the player continues to blow. This makes a very brilliant form of staccato.

Measure 15. It is suggested that the low D# be fingered with the thumb and the 1st finger of each hand (forked fingering). This will make it easier to finger the B. The Bs should be played on the left since the D# can only be fingered on the right. Finger the last note with the chromatic fingering since this will produce the best tone and pitch on the high D# that follows.

Measure 16. The letter M indicates that the middle finger of the right hand should be used. If the chromatic fingering were used it would not be possible to finger the D# that follows.

Measure 17. It is suggested that the first two fingers of the right hand be held down from the B across the G to the E. This is indicated by the sign ⌐⌐ .

Measure 19. It is suggested that the D# be played using the thumb and the 1st and 5th fingers. This makes it much easier to finger the B's that follow these notes.

Measure 21. Fingering the low D# with the thumb and 1st and 5th fingers will make it easier to finger the D# and also the B that follows.

Measure 24. The first note would be fingered with the right little finger on C and the left little finger on B.

Measure 28. The tendency is to not hold the notes out their full value. The note should be held until the second beat begins. The note should also be rounded off with a nice decrescendo.

Measure 29. Note that the staccato marks have stopped. Therefore play in a more legato style.

Measure 36. This is one of the measures with the duple rhythm in a triplet setting. To play this correctly, count three in your mind on each beat as you play so that the triplet rhythm will be felt along with the duple rhythm.

Measure 39. Finger the F# with the chromatic key (T R 1 2 3 4 K). This will make the high D that follows much more easily fingered.

It is very difficult to play the entire exercise either *ff* or *pp,* but the player will be richly rewarded in great dynamic control if he will give this his best effort.

Grade III

Nº 8

STUDY No. 9

This is a delightlful exercise designed to develop finger technique and smoothness. The intervals are very interesting and helpful with a wide variety of intervals involved. There are many places where the right hand down technique can be utilized for greater smoothness. When the exercise has been brought up to the recommended tempo it is believed that the player may breathe at each second breath mark. At slower practice tempos, each phrase mark will probably be needed. The extra breath marks have been circled. These should be eliminated when played up to tempo.

Measure 1. The C natural in this measure should be played with the right little finger. The right hand should be held down across the Bb, A and G.

Measure 2. The tenuto mark over the Eb indicates a climax of this line. Play the Eb a little broader and a little louder.

Measure 10. It is suggested that the right hand be placed down on the second note (Bb) in order to make the passage smoother and more easily played.

Measure 19. Play the first C with the right little finger and the second C with the left little finger.

Measure 20. This tenuto mark over the A is similar to the tenuto mark over the Eb in the second measure. Play the A broader and louder to make a climax to the phrase.

Measure 22. Play the first note (Eb) with the forked fingering (T 1 4). This will make the passage smoother and more easily fingered.

Measure 25. In order to play from Eb to C to Db to Eb, two notes must be played following one another with the same little finger. It is suggested that the Eb and the C be played with the right little finger. This is called a slide. In order to make the slide easier, rub a little oil from the side of your nose on the tip of the right little finger. This will make it easy to slide from one key to another. The signal for the slide is ⌢ .

Measure 27. A similar slide has to be made in this measure. The exact same slide has to be made and should be done in the same fashion as in measure 25.

Measure 30. The forked fingering will help to make the Eb prepare for the Eb that follows.

Measure 32. Placing the right hand down on the Bb will make this passage smoother and easier. The signal for this is R H D.

Measure 34. Start the trill slowly and move gradually faster. Play the grace notes just ahead of the next beat. Keep the right hand C fingering down across the grace note Bb.

Measure 35. Finger the Bb with the second and third fingers of the left hand down to insure a beautiful and resonant Bb. Keep the right hand down across the grace note Bb.

Measure 44. Finger the F# with the chromatic key (T R 1 2 3 4 K). This will make it easier to play the F natural that follows.

Measure 48. In making the octave skip, it helps to use the syllable AH on the first C and EE on the second C. Finger the Bb at the end of the measure with the bottom side key.

Measure 50. This passage will be smoother and more readily played if the high Bb is fingered with the forked fingering (T R 1 4).

Measure 51. Finger the Db with the right little finger on the C key and the left little finger on the C# key.

Measure 61. Trill the A to the Bb using the second side trill key from the top. Play the grace notes just ahead of the beat.

Measure 68. The ritard has been added by the editor to give the exercise a more musical ending.

It is suggested that this and other exercises that lend themselves to a steady tempo be practiced with a metronome. This will help to build a feeling for the inner rhythmical pulse needed for fine performance.

STUDY No. 10

Exercise #10 is excellent for the development of quick nimble fingers. Most of the notes are 32nds and they go by very quickly. It is also a good exercise for the development of time counting. Almost without exception the 32nd notes come on the downbeat attached to a 16th note followed by an 8th note rest. This rhythm must be exact. It is helpful to play a few bars in 8 beats to the measure to get the rhythm exact. Then the exercise can be practiced in 4. It is recommended that a slow 4 with the metronome set at about 76 beats per minute be used in the beginning. Then gradually increase the tempo to Mr. Rose's suggested 126.

Measure 1. In counting the first measure in 8 the first two notes come on the down beat and the third note comes exactly on the up beat. If you were counting it out loud, it would be "Down two up" and the next beat would be a rest. To establish the correct rhythm, it is a good idea to practice at first in 8 beats to the measure using a metronome.
The term "tres legerement" is French. It means to play very lightly and happily.

Measure 2. Play the C with the right little finger and the B by adding the left little finger.

Measure 4. The crescendo and the tenuto marks have been added by the editor. They help to make a more musical return to the original theme. Play the third line B that appears near the end of the measure with the right little finger on C and the left little finger on B.

Measure 8. Play the grace notes lightly and just ahead of the second beat. Finger the F#: T R 1 2 3 5.

Measure 11. Finger the high Eb with the standard fingering (T R 2 3 4 K G#). Then finger the following F# with the same basic fingering (T R 1 2 3 4 K). The K in this fingering stands for the B key.

Measure 12. Placing the right hand down on the throat tone G will make this passage smoother. The sign for this is R H D. Use the chromatic fingering for the F# (T R 1 2 3 4 K). The crescendo and tenuto markings have again been added by the editor to make the study more musical.

Measure 17. Notice that the rhythm has changed. If you are now practicing the study in 4 beats to the measure, it is suggested that you return to counting in 8 to insure correct rhythm. Note that there is also a change of key.

Measure 18. Play the grace notes just ahead of the beat. Do not rush them.

Measure 29. All but the first beat of this measure can be fingered with the right hand down. It will make the second beat easier and smoother if the right hand is placed down on the Bb at the beginning of the beat.

Measure 31. We have another change of rhythm in this measure. If practicing in 8, the two thirty-second notes come on the down beat and the sixteen note rest comes on the up beat. When practicing in 4 the first 32nds come on the down beat and the next group of 32nds are on the up beat.

Measure 32. Finger the high F with what is known as the "long" fingering, (R T 1 2 3 C# 4 5 6). This is a very sure fingering and is often used in moving to high F from a large interval.

Measure 34. There is a misprint in the original music in this measure. The last note of the third and fourth beat were printed as 32nd notes. These errors have been corrected in this edition.

Measure 44. Count the dotted eighth "Down two three" and "four" on the sixteenth note to get this figure in exact rhythm.

Measure 48. It is suggested that the right hand be placed down on the open G to make this run smoother and easier. Tenuto markings have again been added to indicate the return of the original theme. This is known as a recapitulation.

Measure 49. Note the key change. Always pay close attention to the key signature. This is one of the first things one looks at when beginning to play a new piece.

Measure 52. Finger the B in the 3rd beat with the right hand little finger on the C key and the left hand little finger on the B key. Make a small tenuto at the end of the measure in order to point out the recapitulation, which follows in Measure 53.

Measure 54. Play all the Bs in this measure with the right hand little finger on the C key and the left hand little finger on the B key.

Measure 57. Finger the Bbs in the first beat with the side fingering (R T 1 2 Eb).

Measure 61. Notice that this measure is written in the key of F Major. The flat in front of the chalumeau B was omitted in the original addition. It has been added by the editor. An accidental changes only that note and similar notes in the measure. Notes in other octaves are not affected.

Measure 64. This rhythm is similar to that in measure 31. This time the counting is presented in 4 beats per measure.

It is extremely important that the clarinetist practice every day. If a day is missed the rate of progress does not stand still but actually goes backwards.

Grade IV

№ 10

STUDY No. 11

Allegretto is a tempo marking and also a style. It is a little slower than an Allegro (quick or lively) and also is to be played in a happy, joyful style. The exercise is to be played in a slow two beats per measure. When first practicing the exercise it is suggested that it be played in 6 beats per measure and then gradually increase the tempo until two beats per measure with 76 beats per minute is reached.

The purpose of this exercise is to develop staccato tonguing and the ability to play small intervals. It is interesting to note that there is only 1 half measure and 1 full measure that have scale passages in the entire exercise.

Measure 1. In order to obtain the utmost in benefit from the practice of this exercise, the editor has placed dynamic markings alternating between forte and piano for each line. The staccato tonguing should be the style known as stopped staccato.

It is suggested that the B's in the measure be fingered with the C on the right and the B on the left. This prepares the fingers for playing the C that follows on the right. The line over the notes in this and following measures indicates that all or part of the right hand may be left down. This makes for smoother, more fluent technique.

Measure 4. Note that this line is to be practiced at the dynamic level of piano. The first B and the C are to be played with the right little finger. Keeping the fingering in one hand in this manner makes for better more efficient fingering technique. The B at the end of the measure should be fingered with the C on the right and the B on the left. This is the standard fingering for this note and prepares the fingering for C that follows.

Measure 5. The word "simile" refers to the continuation of the tonguing that was used for the first four measures. All notes not slurred will be tongued stopped staccato for the remainder of the piece.

Measure 8. The F# (third note) should be fingered with the chromatic fingering (T R 1 2 3 4 B). This is a very easy fingering to use following the high D. The C# would be fingered with the right little finger which keeps the fingering in this passage in the right hand.

Measure 12. By keeping down fingers 4 and 5 from the E across A, the C# is already partially fingered.

Measure 15. The first B should be fingered with the right little finger on C, and the left little finger on B. All other Bs will be fingered with the right little finger.

Measure 21. The E flat (third note) should be fingered T R 1 2 D#. This is the chromatic fingering played with the key which is found between the 2nd and 3rd fingers. This keeps the fingering for the E flat all in the left hand for excellent coordination.

Measure 23. It is suggested that the left hand C key be held down with the fingers on the right hand to have the second C already prepared.

Measure 24. It is suggested that the high B flats in this measure be fingered T R 1 4. Since these fingers are already down from the preceeding D's, the fingering will be greatly simplified.

Measure 27. The first note, which is an Eb, should be fingered with the thumb fingers 1 and 2 and the bottom side key (T R 1 2 E flat).

Measure 28. There are two ways to finger the high B flat in this passage. They both have advantages and disadvantages. Practice both fingerings and use the one that works best for you. (T R 1 2 E flat) and (T R 1 4).

Measure 30. The F# in this measure should be played with the first finger of the left hand.

Measure 35. The Editor has added the crescendo and decrescendo markings as well as the tenutos to give a little musical variety to the exercise.

Measure 48. The grace notes are to be played following the third beat. Play the third line B with the right little finger. Group the 5 grace notes into a group of two and a group of three. This gives a flourish leading to the climax on the last note.

A poor reed takes the joy out of playing the clarinet . Always strive to have three or four good reeds and rotate them daily.

Grade III

STUDY No. 12

Allegretto is a tempo marking and also the style the composer wishes for the exercise. Allegretto means to play a little slower than an Allegro (lively) and in a happy, joyful style. The study is composed in the key of E minor. It would be helpful if the scale were practiced before playing this exercise. The notes in the scale are E F# G A B C D# E.

The purpose of this exercise is to learn to play broken chordal passages in the key of Em. Almost the entire exercise is broken chords. It is suggested that the exercise be practiced in 6 beats to the measure at first, gradually increasing the tempo into two beats per measure. Finally, 72 beats per minute should be used. The use of a metronome is strongly recommended.

Measure 1. The grace notes that open the exercise, and all other similar grace notes, are to be played lightly, quickly and just ahead of the beat that follows. The B should be fingered with the right little finger on C and the left little finger on B. Playing the following B with the same fingering sets up the fingers to play the C grace note that comes next.

Measure 2. The B and C grace notes would be fingered the same way as the grace notes in the beginning. The second B would be fingered with the right little finger to keep the fingering in the right hand. This is the usual way of fingering this B in chordal passages.

Measure 4. The D# should be fingered with the first finger of the left hand and the second finger of the right hand (T 1 5). This fingering prepares the fingers for the B that follows. Remember to play the next D# with the Eb key. It is suggested that the third line B be fingered with the right little finger on C and the left little finger on the B key. This puts the fingers in a position to play the following C and the grace notes that follow.

Measure 5. The grace notes would be fingered with B on the left and C on the right. The second B in the measure would be fingered similarly so as to set up the fingering of the C in the grace notes that follow. These would be played with the right little finger.

Measure 7. All of the Bs in this measure are played with the right little finger to keep the fingering in one hand. The line over B, G and D indicate that the right hand may be held down across the G to make the fingering of this passage smoother and easier.

Measure 11. The Bs in this measure are fingered with the right little finger on C and the left little finger on B. This makes it possible to finger the Cs on either side on the right to keep these notes fingered in one hand.

Measure 12. See comments in measure 11 for the fingering of B. The C, last note of the measure, should be fingered with the left little finger in order to finger D# on the right.

Measure 15. All of the Fs in this measure are natural. In the original edition the natural sign for the first space F# was left out.

Measure 16. See comments for Measure 11.

Measure 17. The first C# is fingered on the right in order to keep the fingering in one hand. The next B and C# are fingered with the right and left little fingers successively. This is the standard fingering for these two notes in a scale passage in a sharp key. They set the pattern for the D# to be played on the right as often happens.

Measure 18. The "cresc. poco a poco" means to get louder little by little.

Measure 22. While many fingerings can be used to play the D# in this passage, the editor recommends using the chromatic fingering (T 1 2 D#). This is the only fingering that keeps all the fingers used in one hand.

Measure 23. The F# should be fingered with the 1st finger of the left hand.

Measure 26. The D should be trilled to the note above in the key (E). It is a good idea to prepare a long trill like this by starting it slowing and moving it gradually faster.

Measure 30. This passage will be smoother and better coordinated if the Bs and third space C# are all played with the right little finger.

Measure 31. Fingering the D# with the 1st and 5th fingers is the easiest way to finger the D#. It is executed merely by lifting the 2nd and 3rd fingers. Playing the C (last note) on the right makes it possible to finger the B on the left and the D# in the measure that follows on the right.

Measure 32. The last note of the measure should be fingered with the D# key so as to keep the fingering in one hand. (T R 1 2 D#).

Measure 33. It is suggested that the low D# be fingered T, 1 and 5. This makes it very easy to play the B that follows.

Measure 37. The first D# would be fingered with the T 1 and 5 to prepare for the B that follows. The next D# would be fingered on the side, T 1 2 E flat.

Measure 41. Practice this measure without the grace notes to get the correct rhythm. Then, add the grace notes which are played quickly, lightly and without disturbing the basic rhythm.

Measure 46. When playing passages where the right hand is kept down, keep down the number of fingers needed for the note that follows. For instance in this measure, fingers 4 and 5 would be kept down to play the E.

Measure 50. There is a misprint on the last note of this measure in all editions that the editor has examined. The note should be and E instead of an F.

Grade III

Allegretto ♩.=72

No 12

STUDY No. 13

This is one of the most artistic and beautiful of all the studies in the collection. It is also one of the most difficult. It gives the player the opportunity of expressing himself musically to a very high degree.

The adagio is a very slow tempo. It is a good idea to check it with your metronome. The term "Pathetic" has been made famous by Tschaikovsky's Symphony No. 6, "The Pathetique". Pathetique means pathetic ...sad and unhappy. Play the 32nd in the beat before the first measure just ahead of the first note of the first measure.

Measure 1. Since the D# must be played with the right little finger the C# should be played with the left little finger.

Measure 2. Switch to the right little finger for the half note C# so the D# grace note can also be played with the right little finger. These grace notes would be played before the third beat.

Measure 5. "e sostenuto" means to play this passage in a legato sustained fashion. Count the dotted eighth notes "1 2 3" and the 2 32nds on 4.

Measure 6. The "cross sign" before the last note of the measure is a double sharp. It turns the F# into a G.

Measure 7. "largement" means to play this phrase in a full, broad fashion.

Measure 10. It is suggested that the B be fingered with the right little finger on the C key and the left little finger on the B key.

Measure 11. It is suggested that the D# be fingered with the forked fingering (T 1 4) to make it easier to finger the C that follows.

Measure 12. "Dolce" means to play in a sweet, loving style.

Measure 13. It is suggested that the high C# be fingered ½ (roll the first finger of the left hand down to open the first tone hole). This will help to prevent the high C# sounding too loudly or too uncontroled.

Measure 17. This is another place where the high C# can be played with greater control using the half-hole technique.

Measure 18. It is very musical to play the first note of this measure with a breath accent.

Measure 21. The trill in this measure is to Ab as is indicated by the "tr b". Start the trill slowly and get gradually faster.

Measure 22. B# is the same note as C♮. "Animez" means to animate - move ahead.

Measure 23. It is suggested that the second F# be fingered with the thumb and the 2 bottom side keys. E# is the same as F♮. The following F# would be fingered with the first finger of the left hand.

Measure 24. The question always arises as to how long the fermata (hold) should be held. There is no rule for this but the fermata should be held somewhat longer than the note if appears over. The exact length depends on the artistic judgement of the player.

Measure 25. "Andante" means moving. "Con moto" means with motion. Thus it would seem that Rose wanted a tempo a little faster than an Andante. His ♩ = 88 however indicates a normal andante tempo. There is a change of key to Db Major.

Measure 26. Bbb is a B double flat which is played as an A natural. Adding the 2nd and 3rd fingers of the left hand will improve the tone quality of the A. The Gb would be fingered with the thumb and 2 bottom side keys.

Measure 28. The line with the dot under it is a tenuto marking meaning to tongue lightly and play broadly.

Measure 33. The Gb should be fingered "T R 1 2 3 5".

Measure 35. The Db across the A to the C is one of the few places where the right hand may be held down in this exercise.

Measure 39. It is suggested that the Gb be fingered "T R 1 2 3 4 B" to make it easier to get to the F that follows.

Measure 41. It is suggested that the Gb be fingered with the first finger of the left hand.

Measure 42. It is difficult to coordinate the legato tongue with the breath accents. Slow careful practice is required to accomplish this.

Measure 43. Trilling from Eb to F is a difficult trill as it requires the use of three fingers. After the trill has been started using the regular fingering the trill may be continued moving just the second finger of the right hand and keeping down all other fingers.

Measure 46. It is suggested that the Bb be fingered with the "tonal" fingering. That is A plus the 2nd side key from the top.

Measure 49. "Dolcissimo" means to play in a very sweet, soft and delicate fashion.

Measure 53. This is a very effective ending. Play as softly as possible maintaining beautiful tone quality. It is suggested that the last two notes be played with breath attacks. Thus these tones would be started with the air and with no use of the tongue. This is called a "breath attack" and assures a noisless, delicate attack.

Do not leave your clarinet in a parked car on a hot day. The heat is bad for the instrument and may warp the mouthpiece.

Grade IV

№ 13

STUDY No. 14

Allegro Moderato means a moderate Allegro, a little slower than the usual Allegro. Mr. Rose suggests a tempo of ♩ = 112. The ⟨⟩ have been added by the editor to make the exercise more challenging and more musical.

Measure 1. The word "dolce" is Italian and means to play in a sweet, loving fashion. Play the third line B with the right little finger to keep the fingering in one hand. Keep the right hand down across the G at the end of the measure.

Measure 3. Play the third space C with the right little finger. Keep the right hand down where indicated by the sign ⌐⌐ .

Measure 5. The first space F# should be fingered with the first finger of the left hand.

Measure 11. Finger the first note of the measure with the first finger.

Measure 12. The D# should be fingered with the chromatic fingering (T 1 2 D#).

Measure 17. Finger the first and last notes with the forked fingering (T 1 4). Hold the 4th finger across the G and Bb. Hold the 4th finger down across the Bb and G at the end of the measure.

Measure 18. The same fingerings apply to this measure as those indicated in measure 17.

Measure 27. The climax of this phrase is the high C#. This is indicated by the tenuto mark. This note should be played a little louder and a little more broadly.

Measure 33. Finger the F# with the chromatic fingering.

Measure 34. This measure leads back to the return of the music from the beginning of the exercise. Use chromatic fingerings from the low C# to the end of the measure. Make a slight ritard at the end of the measure to point out the return of the original theme.

Measure 35. The return of the original theme is known as the recapitulation.

Measure 39. The high C to middle D to the high D is a difficult passage. Take plenty of time to play these wide intervals. It is suggested that the high D be played half-holed to avoid having the high D pop out too loudly.

Measure 42. The octave interval from middle E to high E is difficult to play. It helps to make it more playable if the high E is half-holed and the sylables "AH" to "EE" are used to play the interval.

Measure 57. The high G may be fingered several ways. The most common is T R 2 4 5 G#. Play the last three notes with a full and resonant sound.

Tone quality is the most important aspect of clarinet playing.   To develop this practice long tones with a crescendo and decrescendo.

Grade III

Allegro moderato ♩= 112.

№ 14

STUDY No. 15

This beautiful exercise is written in the key of D minor. This can be recognized by the notes at the beginning and end as well as the many C#s that appear in the music.

Measure 1. The original music has a slurring error in this measure. It has been corrected. There are errors made in the slurs in other measures as well. These have all been corrected. The style of the music will be enhanced if the slurs following slurs are played legato throughout the exercise.

Measure 4. The triplet indications were omitted from the original music. These have all been added throughout the exercise. The passage is to be played with three notes on the down beat and three notes on the up beat. The staccato notes should be played using stopped staccato.

Measure 5. The sign ⌐⌐ means to keep the right hand down across the throat register.

Measure 9. It is suggested that the right hand be placed down on the first A in the measure. This makes it much easier to play the C that follows.

Measure 17. The first A of the measure is played exactly on the up beat. The last note of the measure should be played with the right little finger.

Measure 18. Once again we have the sixteenth note triplets. They are played with three notes on the down beat and three notes on the upbeat.

Measure 20. Finger the B natural with the right little finger on C and the left little finger on B. This makes the C at the end of the measure fingered with the right little finger.

Measure 33. Keep the right hand down including the C key which would be kept down from the B in measure 32.

Measure 37. Finger the Bb with the side key (T R 1 2 Eb).

Measure 38. The first note needs to be played with the left little finger since the high D requires the right little finger to be on the G# key.

Measure 53. It is suggested that the right hand be placed down on the first note of the measure to make the 4th note C easier to play.

Measure 55. It is suggested that the high Ds be fingered half-holed. This will make this passage smoother and more beautiful.

Measure 61. The C# on the second beat must be played with the left little finger since the right little finger is needed in playing the high D.

Measure 63. The ritard has been added by the editor to give a greater feeling of finality and to make the ending more musical.

It is suggested that the student practice this exercise in four measure units. Start slowly with the first four measures and practice them gradually faster. When the first four measures are up to tempo, work on the next four measures in a similar fashion. Next, put the eight measures together. Now practice the entire exercise using this method.

STUDY No. 16

This exercise is designed to improve the playing of scales and intervals, particularly the interval of the third. There are some passages requiring the playing of two octave intervals. One extremely difficult series of octaves has caused the editor to give a grade III to this exercise. Without this the exercise would probably be rated grade II. The exercise is most enjoyable to play and is one of the most delightful of the entire 40 studies.

Measure 1. This exercise is in the key of F Major. This first measure is typical of the composition with the F major scale sections and scales in thirds. When slur follows slur it is quite musical to play legato.

Measure 3. The third beat can cause rhythmic problems. The tendency is to start too late after the 16th note rest. To enter exactly on time, subdivide the third beat "one, two, three, four". Rest on one and enter exactly on the second part of the beat.

Measure 6. If a breath is needed before measure 8, a quick one can be taken after the first C. Open the corners of the mouth without disturbing the basic embouchure and gasp quickly.

Measure 8. There is a rhythmic problem here that is similar to measure 3. Divide the second beat into four parts. Enter exactly on the second part. It is suggested that the B natural be fingered with the right little finger on C and the left little finger on B.

Measure 9. When there is a long trill it should be prepared by starting it slowly and getting gradually faster. Play the grace notes in the speed of the trill and just ahead of the beat that follows.

Measure 17. This measure contains the first instance where it is recommended that the right hand be held down from the C across the A and back to the C. In the following measure there are four places where the right hand would be held down.

Measure 19. It is suggested that the high Bb be fingered using the forked fingering (R T 1 4). The bridge mechanism must be in adjustment to play this fingering. If the fingering does not work, your clarinet teacher or band director can adjust this mechanism for you.

Measure 20. While most clarinet players realize that they can play back and forth from notes above this throat register, many do not know that the right hand down rule also works for the notes below the throat register. For instance, the last note of measure 19 can have the first finger of the right hand held across the 1st note of the next measure to play the C. The last note of measure 20, low A allows 2 fingers of the right hand be held down across the first three notes of measure 21 to play the E, 4th note of measure 21.

Measure 22. The *sfz* is an abbreviation for sforzando. This is a strong accent. Be sure you make this accent with the breath rather than with the tongue.

Measure 24. Subdivide the first beat playing the C on the downbeat and the G exactly on the upbeat.

Measure 25. Play the three grace notes just before the third beat. Trill from G to the note above in the key (A). Start the trill slowly and get gradually faster. Keep the trill even as you accelerate. Play the last two grace notes just before the first note of the following measure.

Measure 29. The octave intervals should be practiced slowly and carefully. Play them as quarter notes at first. Play gradually faster until they can be played as eighth notes. Then increase the speed until they can be played 16th notes, up to tempo. Take special care to play them in tune.

Measure 30. The ritard has been added by the editor. This measure has a good example of holding the right hand down in the low register across the throat register.

Measure 31. Play the grace note just ahead of the first beat and with a nice flourish!

Always have your clarinet in excellent playing condition. Visiting your repairman every six months is an excellent idea.

STUDY No. 17

This is one of Rose's best studies. It makes use of the short slur and short staccato. For best effect it is recommended that the player use the "stopped" method of making staccato. Here the player stops the tone brilliantly as if saying the word "tut".

Allegretto means less than an Allegro. It is suggest that a tempo of ♩ = 96 be used. It is also recommended that a metronome be used in the practice of this study. Since it has a steady tempo throughout it lends itself very well to the use of a metronome.

Measure 1. The first 2 measures can be played holding part of the right hand down. Play the staccato notes very short.

Measure 5. The right hand plus the little fingers can be held down in this passage.

Measure 6. Hold the first finger of the right hand down across A nd G# in order to finger the F.

Measure 15. Finger the two Bs with the right little finger. The third B should be played with the right little finger on C and the left finger on B.

Measure 18. Here we have a phrasing marking articulation slurs. The player is to observe the slurs closest to the notes. Play these slurs legato.

Measure 21. This is a difficult measure. Practice it very slowly giving each note one beat. To help play the large intervals say "ee-ah" when moving from the high note to the low note.

Measure 27. There is a rhythmical problem here that needs to be counted in order to play the passage exactly right. Practice counting in four beats to the measure. Sixteenth notes then become eighth notes. It would then be counted "down up down 2 3 4 - 2, Down up down 2 3 4 - 2" etc. After you can count the passage correctly, count and finger it. Then play it at the slow tempo. Now increase the tempo until you can play it in two beats per measure.

Measure 35. This passage consists of a series of 32nd and 16th notes coming on the downbeat and upbeat. Be certain to play the 32nd notes very quickly and observe the 32nd rest.

Measure 40. The rhythm is similar on the downbeats and the 2 sixteenth notes appear exactly on the upbeat.

Measure 65. It is suggested that these two measures be practiced first in four beats to the measure. In four, they would be counted "down up down d d down up down d d". The C# grace note would be played with the right little finger. Both of the grace notes would be played quickly and just ahead of the beat that follows. Grace notes receive no time value.

Remove the mouthpiece and dry your clarinet with a cloth swab after each use. Drop the weight in the bell and draw the swab through with a steady pull.

Grade V

Nº 17

STUDY No. 18

This is one of the most difficult exercises in the book. It should be practiced slowly and carefully. Individual measures that need time in working out the counting must be given special attention. The time counting system which uses down and up (with the foot and numbers) is highly recommended. After the time counting has been worked out, practice counting with the foot. Then practice counting and fingering. When this can be done with ease, the student should be ready to play the study.

This beautiful study should be played at an extremely slow tempo. It would undoubtedly be a good idea to practice it first in eight beats to the measure.

The comments here however will be given with the idea that it is being played in four beats to the measure since this is the feeling the music should have. It would be a good idea to use a metronome when practicing this music as the rhythm and time counting are quite difficult.

Measure 4. The trill should start slowly and gradually move more rapidly ending on the C from which it begins. The two grace notes come just before the following beat and are connected to the trill.

Measure 5. Counting the first beat is difficult. There are seven units in the A and the G comes on the eighth unit. Thus the A would be counted "1, 2, 3, 4, 5, 6, 7" and the G would be played on "8".

Measure 7. The trill always moves to the note above in the key unless the note above is altered by an accidental. Thus the E in this case will be trilled to F#.

Measure 9. The second beat should be subdivided to get the rhythm correct. It would be counted "1, 2, 3" and the two 32nd notes would be played on "4". The top mark is for phrasing and indicates one unit. The marks closer to the notes are the articulations.

Measure 10. The four 32nd notes in this measure would all be played exactly on the up beat of the second beat.

Measure 11. Play the slurs on beats three and four with breath accents. Play this passage in a legato style. Use the chromatic fingering for the C# at the end of the measure.

Measure 13. The 32nd notes at the beginning of the measure are played with 8 notes on a beat. It is best to count 4 notes on the down beat and four on the up beat.

Measure 14. The turns in this measure would be played:

This first 8th note and the 32nd note turn would be played on the downbeat and the following two 16th notes would be played on the upbeat.

Measure 15. The third beat of the measure should be divided into 4 units. The dotted eighth note would take up the first three units while the three 32nd notes would be played on the fourth unit. The trill under the hold should be played with a crescendo. The following quarter note D tied to the eighth note D would be played with a decrescendo. The D should be tongued.

Measure 17. The sharp under the turn means that the lower note of the turn would be played with a sharp. Thus the notes of the turn would be E, D, C#, D. These would be played as follows:

Measure 23. To trill the A to B natural, hold the A key down and trill with the top side key. Since the fingering is quite false it is a good idea to start the trill with the regular B fingering and change to the top side key when the trill begins to gather speed. In the original edition the natural sign for the grace note at the end of the measure was left out. Since it obviously should be G♮, the editor has made the correction.

Measure 25. See measure 14 and 17 for information on playing this turn.

Measure 31. See measure 23 for suggestions on playing the trill from A to B. The grace note at the end of this measure has also been corrected to read G♮.

Measure 32. The half note G should be tongued. Bring out the grace notes slightly and die away on the last note. The last note should die away to silence.

In cold weather do not play your clarinet until it has warmed up to room temperature. Otherwise, it may crack.

STUDY No. 19

This is a very demanding broken chord study. It contains many accidentals as well as many fingering problems. There are two passages that require the use of the sliding technique. That is, playing two keys in a row with the same finger. This will be explained in detail when these passages appear in the music.

Measure 9. The last C in the measure should be played with the left little finger to make it easier to get to the Eb in the following measure.

Measure 12. This measure will be played more easily if the Bbs above the staff are all fingered T - R - 1 - 4 (forked).

Measure 13. It is suggested that difficult measures like this be practiced with the 16th notes receiving one beat, then ½ beat and finally played as 16th notes.

Measure 14. The term decrescendo means to get gradually softer .

Measure 18. This is one of the two measures in this exercise that requires the player to use the slide technique. The slide occurs on the last two notes of the measure. The Eb can only be fingered on the right. The Db could be fingered on the left but the C that follows also has to be fingered on the left. The easiest slide is to slide from the Eb to the Db with the right little finger. The sign for the slide is ⤸. If the finger sticks to the keys rub the tip of the right little finger along the side of the nose. The oil gathered on the finger will make a smooth and efficient slide possible.

Measure 21. This is the other measure requiring the slide. Since the Ab's can only be fingered with the left little finger the Eb and C must both be fingered with the right little finger.

Measure 28. The editor has added a ritardando in this measure to point out the return of the original theme.

Measure 29. This is the original theme found at the beginning of Study Number 1. The "a tempo" means to play in the same tempo as was used before it was changed by the ritardando.

Measure 39. The "rit." is an abbreviation for ritardando. This means to play gradually slower. The editor has added this marking to make a more finished and musical ending.

It is important that the mouthpiece be kept clean at all times. Do not run a swab through the mouthpiece as this will in time wear off the sharp edges and ruin the mouthpiece. Clean the mouthpiece by washing it once a week in lukewarm soapy water.

Grade IV

STUDY No. 20

Polonaise ♩ = 104. The Polonaise is a Polish dance written in 3/4 time. Runs, skips and syncopation are characteristics of this music. C. Rose has indeed caught the spirit of the Polonaise in this exciting study.

Measure 1. The grace note E should be played just ahead of the beat. Although the directions are to trill from D to E there is not time to do so. The best way to play this, in the opinion of the editor, would be to play a 32nd note triplet D E and back to D. Playing the C# with the right little finger will keep the fingering of this passage in one hand and thus improve coordination. The sign ⌐ indicates to keep the right hand down across the throat tones G and A. This makes the B much easier to play.

Measure 2. It is suggested that the staccato be made by stopping the tone with the tongue. This results in a brilliant staccato effect. Note the phrase or breath mark in the measure. The D must be shortened in order to have time to take a quick breath. Be certain to observe the accent above the Eb with an extra burst of air to make the beginning of the note slightly louder.

Measure 3. The figure of a sixteenth note slurred to a thirty-second note is played like 2 sixteenth notes with the second one shortened each time the figure occurs.

Measure 14. To get the rhythm exact on the second beat, subdivide into 4 parts or sixteenths. The eighth note will get the value of the first 2 sixteenths, the sixteenth rest will get the 3rd sixteenth and the sixteenth note the 4th sixteenth.

Measure 20. It is suggested that the B be fingered with the right little finger on the C key and the left little finger on the B key.

Measure 37. Note the key change to C Major.

Measure 40. The last three notes of this measure are tongued legato. Make the tongue as light as possible and keep the air moving between the notes. Use the chromatic fingering for the F# (T R 1 2 3 4 K).

Measure 47. The *sfp* stands for sforzando-piano. This is a large accent. Following the sforzando the note is immediately held softly. The same type of accent is found in measure 53.

Measure 56. The grace notes in this measure should be played just ahead of the upbeats. The Ds are played exactly on the up beats. The last note should be played with the left little finger so the Eb in the following measure can be played with the right little finger.

Measure 64. Use the chromatic fingering of the D# (R T 2 3 4 K G#). Play these high notes as if pronouncing the syllable "eee".

Measure 68. This is the recapitulation where the exercise returns to the music at the beginning. Play in the same style as at the beginning.

Measure 75. The style of the exercise changes at this point. Measure 75 should be played legato. When slur follows slur they are nearly always played legato.

It is hoped that the clarinetist has enjoyed studying the master lesson plans written for these very fine studies by C. Rose. Hopefully the player has profited by the many comments and suggestions found in this edition of the Studies. The editor wishes you a lifetime of successful and enjoyable clarinet playing.

NOTES ON CLARINET FINGERINGS

Throughout this book, the clarinet fingerings are labeled according to the following system:

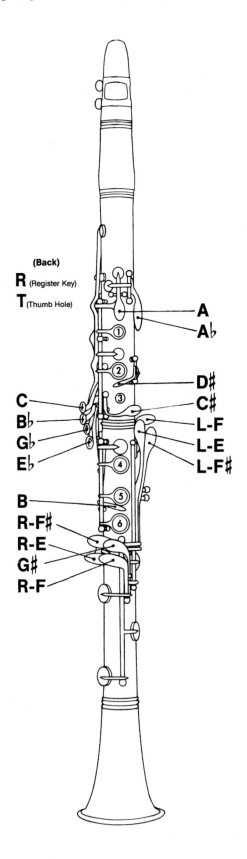

The finger holes are numbered 1-6. The register key is indicated by the letter R, while the thumb hole is indicated by the letter T. The remaining keys are labeled according to the pitches that they produce.